sergio rossi

© 2008 Assouline Publishing
601 West 26th Street, 18th floor
New York, NY 10001, USA
Tel.: 212 989-6810   Fax: 212 647-0005
www.assouline.com

Translated from French by Sylvie Kleiman-Lafon

ISBN: 978 2 7594 0170 3

Color separation: Gravor (Switzerland)
Printed by Grafiche Milani (Italy)

sergio rossi

ANNE-MARIE CLAIS

ASSOULINE

t hat evening, Eva Longoria was wearing a short printed-muslin dress with a plunging neckline. She walked decidedly, perched high on a pair of delicate sandals that put the final touch to her flawless figure. These sandals, clad in silver lamé from heel to toe, were about to walk up the famous red carpet: this was in Cannes, during the 59th film festival, and Eva Longoria was about to climb the stairs.

This happened in May 2006. The sandals bore Sergio Rossi's signature, as did all the outstanding shoes worn that day by Sharon Stone, Aishwaraya Rai, Diane Kruger, Michelle Yeoh, Faye Dunaway, Ludivine Sagnier, Zhang Ziyi and Miranda Richardson. Photographers were everywhere, and so were journalists from around the world. However surprising it may sound, they were all about to discover that the stars, encouraged by protocol, were not barefoot contessas. With the cameras as witnesses, the Italian brand was revolutionizing the world of fashion: accessories were officially coming into their own, after centuries of discreet complicity with clothing.

Black and white débuts

Just like any pre-credits scene, this one calls for a flashback. The scene takes place in Italy, just after the war: San Mauro Pascoli is a small village of less than four thousand inhabitants, in Emilia-Romagna. On the map, it is an enclave in an ancient land, where place-names remind us of the Rubicon and the Via Emilia. It has long been an agricultural region. Its territory is a narrow corridor leading to the Adriatic sea, pointing towards San Mauro a Mare: a promise of eternal sunshine merely four miles away from the village square. The Italian poet Giovanni Pascoli was born in this rustic land in 1855. Champion of a simple, though arduous, way of life close to nature, he wrote poems of melancholy celebration. As in so many parts of Italy, a major episode in Italian history happened here. In this traditionally rural economy, a small craft industry developed into a booming activity, prompting social changes and encouraging a swiftly increasing consumption. In San Mauro Pascoli the metamorphosis was induced by the production of shoes, as it was by the textile industry anywhere else. At a time of vast possibilities, the village experienced unprecedented development, which brought with it the prospect of a better future, the end of the dark years, and a more comfortable life for all. Thanks to the favours of history and human energy, a whole generation finally had access to what had looked like an impossible dream to the previous one. Sergio Rossi was one of those who dared carry their dreams further.

Great adventures are very often lived by adults who were deprived of their childhoods. Out of this simple and universal plot, the cinema has produced a masterpiece: Citizen Kane. The story of Sergio Rossi is far from being so extreme: Italy was then so different from America! But these elements are the basis on which legends are made. Few details of Sergio Rossi's childhood are known, but one can imagine it like a series of black and white images, in the neo-realistic vein of the Italian cinema of the 1940s and 1950s: soft light, restrained dialogues and familiar settings where all mothers look like Anna Magnani.

As any child, young Sergio Rossi invented his own future: he too had a dream. His dream was no more foolish than any other boy's: he wanted to become a stationmaster, just like his uncle. One may easily guess the images that endlessly scrolled through his young head: the classic images of the history of cinema since the Lumière brothers and their *Train Arriving at the Station in La Ciotat*. The steam engine shrieks in a cloud of smoke; one can hear the hurrying footsteps of travellers, doors being slammed, and the sound of a whistle. The train pulls away without revealing its mysterious destination: it has to be far-off and thrilling.

But, as everyone knows, childhood dreams rarely come true. Sergio Rossi never became a stationmaster: he was not meant to stay behind on the platform, as he painfully came to understand.

The dreams of this child of San Mauro Pascoli were thwarted by reality and he was soon forced into wearing the loose suit of a responsible adult. His father was a shoemaker: following his footsteps, he embraced this hereditary occupation, both out of duty and out of necessity, to learn the trade and sustain his family. When his father died in 1949, he was only fourteen, and already knew all the tricks of the trade. He had spent his whole childhood and youth watching his father. However, one should probably not speak of the transmission of knowledge. Sergio Rossi *took* this knowledge more than it was *given* to him. He watched all the gestures, the expertise, and the tricks that had become automatic movements — something one knows without having ever learnt. Throughout these years of discreet observation he developed a photographic eye, a memory filled with images and sequences covering all aspects of the trade, and the mysteries of hand-made objects. He reproduced them and then enriched them, as though he had been reciting a lesson learnt by heart. This modest start in life, shaped by acceptance and by the burden of tradition is typical of post-war Italy, where the sense of reality mattered more than anywhere else. Back then, in Italy, people were, above all, pragmatic, ready to grasp opportunities and chances whenever circumstances allowed it. The story of Sergio Rossi begins as a simple story, that of a man who strove to make the most out of the values of hard work, expertise, quality and craftsmanship that made the reputation of shoes "made in Italy". It is also the story of a man who believed in his own future and in the many possibilities that were offered, at the time, to society as a whole. It is the story of a family man, who started the adventure with his brother Franco, six years his junior, who became his director of production.

To dare to dream further

In 1958, the first technologically advanced building of industrial size entirely dedicated to the shoe industry was erected in San Mauro Pascoli. It is called *Mir Mar*, as an invitation to look farther away, towards the sea. More than San Mauro a Mare, Rimini, the neighbouring seaside town, had already been for quite a while the bustling cosmopolitan dream of many a conquering spirit. Fellini was born there and paid tribute to his hometown in his film *Amarcord*, a collection of memories that came out in 1973. In the film, Tita, a teenager, learns the lessons of life by observing guests at the Grand Hotel, for whom he invents imaginary lives. Maybe Sergio Rossi had met them on the platform of a train station. Maybe the train of his childhood was like the Ocean liner in *Amarcord*, and left with a promise.

The time to look beyond the border had not come yet. Everything happened in Italy. In Rome, the success of Cinecitta, *Hollywood sul Tevere*, attracted the Americans. Their presence gave the capital an international dimension, taking Florence in its wake. Haute Couture developed, paving the way for a radical change in the history of fashion, which, until then, had not existed outside Paris. As early as 1951, in his private residence in Florence, Marquis Gian Battista Giorgini organized Alta Moda's first fashion show. The success was such that the show moved to the Palazzo Pitti and adopted the schedule of the Parisian shows. There, Gucci showed his first pedal-pushers, Valentino imposed his patrician elegance before he opened his first workshop in Rome. They created an Italian alternative to Parisian Haute Couture. Rome became a movie star and celebrated la *dolce vita*: Fellini gave his famous film in 1960, won the Palme d'Or at the Cannes film festival, and Antonioni filmed *La Notte* in 1961. Their female characters have the beauty of the devil. They are called Monica Vitti, Anouk Aimé, Anita Ekberg, or Jeanne Moreau. The tide had finally turned: when fashion was made in Paris, the city attracted Italian designers such as Schiaparelli or Nina Ricci. All the French actresses suddenly dreamed of making films in Italy.

To Sergio Rossi, Rome was still very far away. At the beginning of the 1950s, he went to Milan to study and train. The word *design* had not yet replaced *conception*. In Milan, he learned how to make the most of his passion for shapes, the very heart of the shoemaker's know-how, and he went further in his apprenticeship two years later — he was then twenty — with a Master in Bologna.

Concentrating on his work, he was not yet attracted by the paparazzi spirit, so typical of Rome and of Italy's revival. Indifferent to this permanent agitation, he soon started to sell his models to shops in Bologna and spent his winters making sandals he would later sell, in the summer, on the beaches of Rimini. One of these sandals proved decisive. The model was called Opanca. The design was both simple and daring: the sole was gently curved around the foot so as to blend itself with the upper part of the shoe. A journalist from Merano noticed it and came back a year later to introduce Sergio Rossi to a German associate. The man was enthusiastic and soon talked of manufacturing twenty to thirty thousand pairs a year. The modest craftsman alone could hardly face the demand. Sergio Rossi started to dream of establishing a factory. It was inaugurated in 1966 in spite of an unkept promise: the German investor backed out at the last minute and the factory was born on "a heap of debts".

Rome was becoming a movie star and Milan was brewing a revolution

despite Rome's Alta Moda, young designers started in Milan what was to prompt the triumph of Italian ready-to-wear. This mixture of audacity and freshness was brightly illustrated by Walter Albini, Krizia or Missoni. It all started with the opening of Elio Fiorucci's boutique, a kitsch and pop place in the spirit of swinging London. At the same time, impetuous young architects were inventing modern design: Gae Aulenti, Ettore Sottsass, Lino Zanussi, and many others. The whole nation was then

10

torn between tradition and avant-garde, the provinces and the Rome-Florence alliance, the old world and the new one. The Ancients and the Moderns played in different keys. The end of the story is well known.

At a time when everything was changing, Gianni Versace was still an apprentice. During the 1960s he learned his trade in his mother's workshop in Calabria. Gianni Versace and Sergio Rossi: two parallel destinies that were naturally bound to cross each other's paths. They both inherited an expertise that they knew how to transcend. They both preferred working on volumes to drawing, improving what would later become their signature: the link between body and clothes for the former; the link between body and shoe, conceived as the extension of the leg, for the latter. These common characteristics are not anecdotal, and they partially explain their future collaboration, which contributed to establishing the foundations of a modern Italian luxury that was influenced by neither Rome nor Florence. This casual and sexy chic slowly distinguished itself from the old Roman patrician elegance. It imposed provincial Italy as the authentic purveyor of creations that never gave up quality. This deeply meaningful geography, based on regions, conditioned Sergio Rossi's universe. Born in Emilia-Romagna, he soon became Milanese because of his passion for fashion and its many adventures.

1968:
The first Sergio Rossi shoes

the founding episode was one of extreme tension: in 1968, the whole country was suddenly confronted by an intense social turmoil heralding the armed struggle advocated by the extreme left-wing groups. In 1969, a bomb exploded in Milan, killing sixteen people. A year later, the Red Brigades claimed their first terrorist attack: Italy entered a period in its history that would later be known as the *leaden years*. It was thus in the difficult context of a major political crisis that Sergio Rossi signed his first shoes: a name written in block letters, and a logotype as simple as a child's drawing, affixed to a black round-tipped shoe. Its simplicity offered a stark contrast with the surrounding violence, which reached its apex on May 9, 1978, when Aldo Moro, leader of the Christian Democrats, was murdered after fifty-five days of captivity. In San Mauro Pascoli, a street bears his name. The town itself has a history of violence: the poet that gave it half of its name saw his father murdered.

From these troubled years, the cinema has kept precious memories, such as Lucchino Visconti's cinematic testament, *Conversation Piece*, in which the political plot is combined with the conflict of generations, expressed by the opposition between modern design and the paintings of the old Masters. The era bore the colors of revolution: red like the violence exposed in the photographs of magazines, red like the impossible passion conveyed in Antonioni's film *Red Desert* in 1964.

In its own manner, Sergio Rossi's brand expressed the collective unconscious which later reappeared, once the wounds of Italian history had healed. In the advertising campaigns of the 1990s, red was a tenuous thread, recurring in images that seemed to come out of an Alfred Hitchcock movie. The staging is impeccable and worthy of a movie: windows are smashed, doors are slammed, and oppositions are underlined in red and black, suggesting some dark eroticism. Nothing is said, everything is left to the imagination, as on the poster of Pedro Almodovar's film, *High Heels*, which dates from 1991.

A Passion for images: Technicolor success

a dvertising, however, was a late discovery. Because it was too expensive in the 1970s, an alternative solution had to be found, a process allowing for communication at lower costs without having to abandon a growing ambition. Sergio Rossi was quickly adopted by the booming world of Milanese fashion. He soon became the designers' favourite. They had noticed his exceptional eye, his acute sense of what was in the air, or rather, of what would be. Sergio Rossi became their privileged partner. In Milan, during the shows, everyone would ask him to select shoes for the models on the catwalks, and he could hardly keep up with the demand. He even had to turn down some of the numerous requests he was presented with. Versace, Dolce & Gabbana, or Azzedine Alaïa were among those to whom he said yes. The Milanese fashion shows were a priceless showcase. All the press was there to witness the revival of fashion, in which Italy played the leading part. Sergio Rossi was at the forefront. Each show was a carefully planned spectacle in which the names of the cast are always given. In the press packs, the names of all the craftsmen that worked backstage were duly credited, like in a film, put forward by the prestige of the designers that acted as master-builders. Sergio Rossi's name was on those lists. Most of the shoes of this fashion — which had turned into a spectacle — bore his signature. Thanks to an enthusiastic international press, eager to distill photos and commentaries in the pages of magazines or on television screens, this spectacle became increasingly popular, appealing to audiences worldwide. To have one's name on a press pack handed out in Milan, during the fashion shows, was then the best means to gain a reputation. It was the best publicity a brand could dream of. This is how Sergio Rossi quickly made himself known and imposed shoes as the essential accessories of clothes and fashion.

A period of expansion soon followed. In 1980, in Ancona, he opened the first boutique bearing his name, soon followed by Turin, Florence, Rome, Brussels, New York, Los Angeles, and London. An average of one to two boutiques opened each year between 1980 and 1999. In the meantime, the brand inaugurated a show-room in Milan, in 1995: an indispensable address for any actor of Italian fashion. More than a symbol, it was an accolade.

Success was there, and gave the brand the means to achieve its ambitions. The numerous advertising campaigns gave a more precise image of women according to Sergio Rossi, an image that was indivisible from an era, from a moment in social history. The Italian society had changed tremendously and so had the place assigned to women. Women's image had also evolved, far from the photograph taken from *Bitter Rice* — a film made by Giuseppe De Santis in 1949 — showing Silvana Mangano as the first sex symbol of post-war Italy. She was buxom and represented an ideal of desirability: absolute femininity. In the 1990s, top models came to replace the stars from Hollywood or Cinecitta as the new icons. Overexposed by the media, the star-models imposed a new standard and a new image of the female body: a supple and slender body, thin as a whip, and characterized by long legs. They became Helmut Newton's favourite subject, photographed

14

in low-angle-shot to make theses idols look even taller. Newton himself went so far as to sit in high heels on a sundeck for a self-portrait in which the photographer mimics his own subject.

I n his quest for inspiration, Sergio Rossi could be said to have followed the steps of the Master, born in Berlin ten years before him. They both aspired to get as close as possible to women in order to understand their desires — therein lies Sergio Rossi's secret. He spent long hours, at night, after work, watching women in shoe shops as they were trying on shoes. He wanted to see their eyes in the mirrors to understand what they had to say, or even better, what they did not say. His keen eye was his talent: always alert, he knew how to observe attitudes and movements, and find the perfect alliance between legs and shoes. From this patient observation he drew his own formula: a shoe that is an integral part of the woman who wears it. He gave many illustrations of it: pumps made of carefully adjusted strips of leather and tightly wrapped around the feet, stretch boots, leather laces crossing the ankle. His philosophy was simple: to create nice *shapes* while others dream of creating nice feet. There lies the secret. To think of a shoe, not as a *superimposed* ornament, but as the *continuation* of the body, well-adjusted, comfortable, cosmetic, designed for the movement that befits contemporary women. His style banned ornaments, too often unmotivated, and preferred the pure lines that put shapes forward. Shoes were nearly always one colour and designed as the natural extension of the body. Sergio Rossi was truly in love with shapes. It has been said that whenever he wanted to make a precious gift to someone, he would give a simple signed wooden last, as the starting point of creation.

The numerous images of the advertising campaigns were a tribute to Helmut Newton, with whom Sergio Rossi shared his very contemporary vision of women: an image of forcefulness, of control over the body and its power that points to a change of status. Like the artist, the brand also came to use low-angle-shots to underline the verticality of the body, insisting on the importance of the heel — at least three inches high — which gives the leg its crucial energy and the female body its new stature. The woman fills up the whole space giving the full measure of a seduction that takes power as much as it gives it.

In Milan, Sergio Rossi has always been extremely good at turning the most coveted top models into his accomplices. Seated on a couch, dressed in pantyhose and a simple leotard, Carla Bruni wears Sergio Rossi boots. Her lean body, underlined by the black colour of her clothes, is stretched out on a panther skin. Looking at her, one may wonder if fashion has liberated women or if shoes have freed her from the tyranny of clothes. Accessories have become essential.

Full light and *Full Sun*

t he scene takes place at the turn of the century, in 1999. The landscape has thoroughly changed: the village of San Mauro Pascoli now has more than nine thousand inhabitants, its population has more than doubled in half a century. More than three hundred people work for Sergio Rossi SpA, two thirds of them employed at the factory. Distribution is done through a network of fifteen boutiques directly owned by the company in Europe and in the United States, to which eight franchises were added, located in

Central and Eastern Europe, in the Middle East and in Asia. Thirty years after the creation of the first shoes bearing his name, Sergio Rossi's success is obvious and measurable, enough to attract the attention of the greatest actors in the theatre of fashion.

In 1999, on November 20, Domenico De Sole and Tom Ford finalized the acquisition of the Sergio Rossi brand by the Gucci Group. Through this important change, a symbolic alliance was sealed: that of patrician Italy — Gucci was born in 1921 in Florence — and of the revolutionary Italy represented by Milan. The old rivalry had subsided and the essence was preserved: Sergio Rossi remained Italian. Two elements, however, encouraged dreams of international development: the prestige of the new share holder, quoted on the Stock Exchange since 1995, and that of star designer Tom Ford, who was born in Texas and had become a citizen of the whole world. The list of the new boutiques is long and the locations prestigious: London, Tokyo, Los Angeles. The style became international under the impulse of Tom Ford, who finally left the Gucci Group in 2004 with the professed ambition of confronting Hollywood studios with his talent. Fashion's boy wonder was attracted to cinema.

At Sergio Rossi, Edmundo Castillo took over as designer. Born in Puerto Rico, he had also relinquished his childhood dream of becoming an airline pilot! But his life, not to say his destiny, has never been constrained. Edmundo Castillo was born in a world of shoes: his mother, his sisters and his aunts were crazy about them. His childhood memories were punctuated with the sharp noise of the stilettos the ladies exchanged, collected and cherished. But becoming a shoe designer was nonetheless an exotic choice for the child from Puerto Rico. In his close circle, one could hardly find a master figure. This is not surprising: on the island, no one designs shoes. The advice he received from his sisters, from his friend and fashion illustrator Antonio Lopez, and even more so his passion for fashion triumphed over his initial desire. He was no longer eager to become an airline pilot; he no longer wanted to spend his life in a uniform! As for his passion for travel, this citizen of the world who willingly came to live in Milan confesses that it may be satisfied in many other ways.

Edmundo Castillo knows better than anyone else the particular attraction women have for their shoes. The hidden desires of his customers are no secret to him. He learnt his craft after having studied style at the *Altos de Chavon School of Design*, in the Dominican Republic, and at the *Parsons School of Art and Design* in New York. Above all, he seized the opportunity to put his knowledge into practice and went to work for Donna Karan, in New York. His nine years of experience with her were only interrupted by a short stint working for Ralph Lauren. He always says he owes everything he knows to Donna Karan. He trained his eye in her studio, listened to her advice, and understood the doubts and certainties of a woman of fashion. For her, he travelled along the roads of Italy, looking for the best craftsmen, becoming familiar with a manufacturing process and with the *made in Italy* culture. In 1998, New York's hectic life prompted him to engage in a more personal adventure: he then launched his own line of shoes and managed to impose his own signature. Three years before he joined Sergio Rossi, widely acclaimed by the press and adored by the stars, he was awarded the Perry Ellis Prize for the best accessory designer, granted by the prestigious *Council of Fashion Designers of America*.

From his youth in Puerto Rico he has retained a series of brightly coloured snapshots and a *Full Sun* style made of eager sensuality, refreshing vitality, and opulent spontaneity. He has brought to Sergio Rossi's brand an array of solar colours, a natural taste for textures that flatter both the eye and the hand. To him, shoes are a feast and he never turns down ornaments if they are linked to a function. He thinks as a designer and refuses unmotivated additions. To think of a

18

shoe as a *functioning whole*, such is Edmundo Castillo's obsession. Drawing, which was once his first inclination, has remained the secret laboratory where he structures his collections, for which the attention he pays to the whole never gives precedence to the specific.

h e clearly remembers that his débuts were marked by the reading of a book entitled *The Sex Life of the Foot and the Shoe*, but he does not claim any fetishist tendencies, only the work-ethic of a specialist. His memory is filled with pairs of sandals and pumps he associates with life as it is, a life of friendship and whispered secrets. No wonder he is so enthusiastic about internationally famous American TV series, where one comes across Jennifer Aniston or Eva Longoria in high heels. He is the ambassador of a flamboyant nature enhancing a lively femininity, naturally seductive, born to shine under the sun in Cannes or elsewhere.

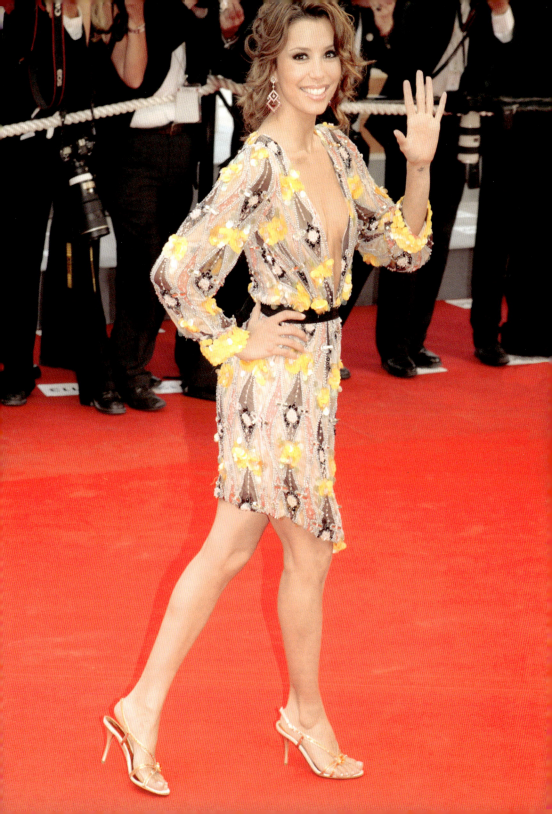

sergio rossi

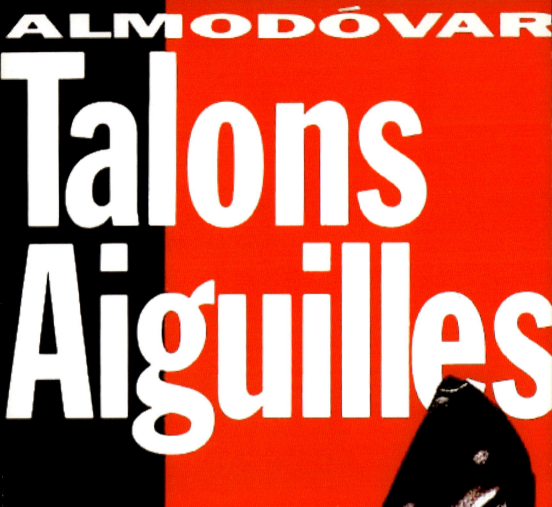

ALMODÓVAR

Talons Aiguilles

VICTORIA ABRIL

MARISA PAREDES

MIGUEL BOSÉ

estate 2007

Sergio Rossi

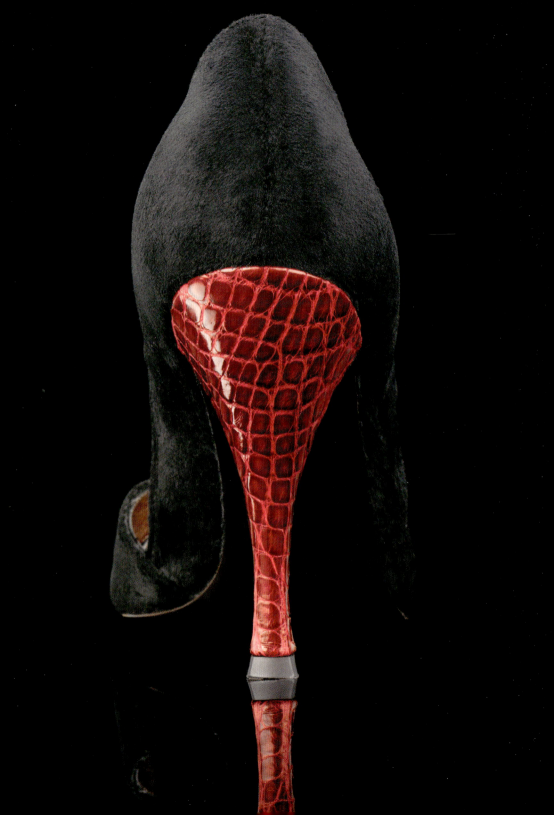

Chronology

1935: Birth of Sergio Rossi on July 31.

1949: Death of Sergio Rossi's father.

1953: Sergio Rossi, aged 18, is in Milan taking classes in model conception.

1955: At the age of 20, he is in Bologna where he is taught by a Master of shapes.

1958: *Mir Mar*, the first technologically advanced building entirely dedicated to the shoe industry is erected in San Mauro Pascoli.

1960: Fellini's *La Dolce Vita* is awarded the Palme d'Or at the Cannes International Film Festival.

1966: *Opanca* sandal.
The first Sergio Rossi manufacture is built.

1968: First shoes bearing Sergio Rossi's signature.
First logotype.

1969: A bomb explodes in Milan, killing sixteen people. Beginning of the *leaden years*.

1970's: First licenses, including Versace.

1973: Fellini's *Amarcord* is a tribute to the filmmaker's childhood in Rimini.

1976: Miss Rossi collection.

1978: May 9, Aldo Moro is murdered after having been held a prisoner for fifty days.

1980: First Sergio Rossi boutique in Ancona. From this date until 1999, the brand opened about two boutiques a year.
The Barbarella line is launched.

1980's: First advertising campaigns.

1982: Opening of a new boutique in Turin.

1983: Opening of a new boutique in Riccione.

1985: Opening of a new boutique in Bologna.
A new line, aiming at younger customers, is launched: the Tini.

1988: Opening of two new boutiques in Milan.

1989: Beginning of collaboration with Dolce & Gabbana, which will last until 1999.

1990's: A collection of bags is launched.
Advertising campaign inspired by Helmut Newton.

Black velvet open toe pump with red crocodile details, Fall/Winter 2006-2007 collection.
© Sergio Rossi.

1993: Opening of a new boutique in Florence.

1994: First boutique in Paris.
Opening of a new boutique in Düsseldorf.

1995: Sergio Rossi opens a show room in Milan.

1996: Opening of a corner in Paris, in the Galeries Lafayette department store.
Opening of a boutique in Rome.

1997: Opening of a new boutique in Savignano.
Opening of a new boutique in Brussels.
Second boutique in Paris.

1998: Opening of a new boutique in New York.
Collaboration with Martine Sitbon.

1999: Launching of a line of shoes for men, under the Echo label.
November 20: Domenico De Sole and Tom Ford finalize the acquisition of the brand
Sergio Rossi by the Gucci Group.

2000: Opening of the first boutique in Japan.

2001: Opening of a new boutique in Los Angeles.
Opening of a new boutique in Venice.

2003: Inauguration of the new manufacture.

2004: Tom Ford and Domenico De Sole leave the Gucci Group.

2006: Presentation of the first collection designed by Edmundo Castillo, Creative director
of the Women Footwear Lines.
A Sergio Rossi showroom is set up in Cannes for the duration of the International
Film Festival.
Opening of the 19th Sergio Rossi store in Japan.
Opening of the first store in China, in Beijing.

2007: Opening of a new boutique in London.
Opening of two Si Rossi corners in Japan.

22 carat gold laminated crocodile pump, Spring/Summer 2007 collection.
© Tommaso Sartori/Bird Production.

sergio rossi

Anita Ekberg in *La Dolce Vita* by Federico Fellini, 1959. © Collection Christophe L.
Eva Longoria wearing gold satin sandals crystal details, Spring/Summer 2006 collection . © Stéphane Feugère.

Hand painted water snake pumps, Spring/Summer 2007 collection. © Sergio Rossi.
In the Sergio Rossi's fabric. © Sergio Rossi.

Ball in Centro Fly, Milan (Italy), 1966. © Toni Nicolini/Azibul.

August 1981, on the Rimini beach (Italy), rows of parasols and folding chairs. © Jonathan Blair/Corbis.
Opanca sandal, 1966. © Sergio Rossi.

Naomi Campbell seen by Albert Watson, wearing black leather ballerinas. Picture in *Vogue* Italy in April 1989. © Albert Watson.
The Italian actress Silvana Mangano during the shooting, in 1954, of Robert Rossen's film, *Mambo*. © Studio Patellani/Corbis.

Silvana Mangano in *Conversation Piece* by Luchino Visconti (1974). © Photos12. com/Collection Cinéma.
Brown sandals with ankle strap, advertising campaign Fall/Winter 2005-2006 collection. © Tom Munro/MAO.

Stage from the film *La Dolce Vita* by Federico Fellini (1959). © Collection Christophe L.
Black patent pump, advertising campaign Fall/Winter 1994-1995 collection. Model: Nadia Aldridge. © Bruno Bisang.

Sergio Rossi's first brand logo. © Sergio Rossi.
Lizard **loafer**, light brown loafer with backle, 60's. © Sergio Rossi.

Black pumps with stod, advertising campaign Fall/Winter 2002-2003 collection. © Guido Mocafico/Katja Martinez Agency.
Monica Vitti on the roof of the Queen Elizabeth Concert Hall palace in London, during the shooting (26th October 1967) of the film *The Girl with the Pistol* by Mario Monicelli. © Rue des Archives.

Laetitia Casta in boots seen by Arthur Elgort, picture published in *Vogue* Italy in November 1994. © Arthur Elgort.
Brown suede boot top chain and brown suede lining, Fall/Winter 2006-2007 collection. © Sergio Rossi.

Ivana Bastionello IV by Gian Paolo Barbieri, picture published in *A History of Fashion – Photographic work 60 & 70* by Gian Paolo Barbieri. © Gian Paolo Barbieri.
The model Waris Dirie seen by Walter Chin, wearing fuxia velvet pump with buckle. Picture published in *Vogue* Italy in September 1992. © Walter Chin/Icon International.

Yellow and violet mini-boots with zip. Picture by Albert Watson published in *Vogue* Italy, in October 1991. © Albert Watson.

Blue velvet ballerinas. Picture by Gian Paolo Barbieri published in *Vogue* Italy, in May1990. © Gian Paolo Barbieri.

Movie poster from *Talons Aiguilles* by Pedro Almodovar. © All Rights reserved.
Black leather strappy sandal. Advertising campaign Spring/Summer 2001 collection. © Mert Alas et Marcus Piggott/Art Partner.

Black leather boot with square heel. Advertising campaign Fall/Winter 2001-2002 collection. © Mert Alas et Marcus Piggott/Art Partner.
Black leather boot with buckle. Advertising campaign Fall/Winter 2001-2002 collection. © Mert Alas et Marcus Piggott/Art Partner.

Brown and white patent leather platform sandals, advertising campaign Spring/Summer 2006 collection. Model: Brenda Costa/Elite. © Benedict Redgrove/Balcony Jump.
Black pumps, end of the 80's. Picture by Satoshi Saikusa, published in *Vogue* Italy in September 1989. © Satoshi Saikusa/Seed.

Black patent leather boot with buckle, Fall/Winter 2006-2007 collection. © Sergio Rossi.
Black loafers with heel, advertising Campaign Spring/Summer 1997 collection. © Marino Parisotto/West Artists.

(Left) Black patent pumps with buckle; (right) black patent pumps with bow. Picture by Patric Shaw published in *Vogue* Italy in September 1995. © Patric Shaw/CLM.
Black patent and suede cage sandal, Spring/Summer 2007 collection. © Sergio Rossi.

Silver sandals with high heel and ankle bow, advertising campaign Spring /Summer 2003 collection. Model: Lisa M. © Solve Sundsbo/Art and Commerce.
Metallic leather toe platform pump with Plexiglas heel, Fall/Winter 2006-2007 collection. © Sergio Rossi.

Sketch of a model of a gold satin rope sandal with pearl beaded straps. Spring/Summer 2007 collection. © Sergio Rossi.
Brown sandals with ankle strap and fur bobble, advertising campaign Fall/Winter 2000-2001 collection. © Richard Burbridge/Art and Commerce.

Brown leather strappy sandals, advertising campaign Fall/Winter 2000-2001 collection. © Richard Burbridge/Art and Commerce.
Sketch of a model of a silver cage sandal. Spring/Summer 2007 collection. © Sergio Rossi.

Bronze leather boots with high heel, advertising campaign Fall/Winter 2006-2007 collection. © Richard Burbridge/Art and Commerce.

Sequinned pumps with grosgrain around the ankle, advertising campaign Spring/Summer 2006 collection. Model: Brenda Costa. © Benedict Redgrove/Balcony Jump.

Black patent leather small *Vanity* handbag and black suede platform sandal with gold rings, advertising campaign Spring/Summer 2007 collection. Model: Tella Soone. © Miles Albridge/D and V Management.

Brown pumps with micro leather strap, advertising campaign Fall/Winter 2003-2004 collection. © Solve Sundsbo/Art and Commerce.
Black leather pumps with high heel and ankle strap, advertising campaign Fall/Winter 2003-2004 collection. © Solve Sundsbo/Art and Commerce.

Veronica **model**, patent leather pumps in different colours and materials, Spring/Summer 2007 collection. © Sergio Rossi.

Acknowledgements

The author sincerely wishes to thank the house of SERGIO ROSSI, and more particularly Isabelle Guichot, Didier Bonnin and Xavier Rougeaux for the active memory they so willfully share and for the warm attention they have given to this work, Angela Di Mento, and all the staff at SERGIO ROSSI who have generously accepted to share their memories about the brand.
She also wishes to thank Eloïse Didier, Ginevra Boralevi and Cristina Paparozzi, and Sylvie Kleiman-Lafon.

The Publisher wants to thank Serge Darmon (Christophe L Collection), Stéphane Feugère, Liza Anderson, Giovanna Burinato (Azibul), Isabelle Martin (Corbis), Aaron Watson, Claudine Zuzinec (Photos 12), Silvia (Management Artists), Ken Nguyen (Rex Photographic), Bruno Bisang, Christophe Chalvet de Recy (Profile Model Management), Marie-Jeanne Baqué (Katja Martinez Agency), Catherine Terk (Rue des Archives), Marianne Houtenbos (Arthur Elgort), Phil Sanders (Allarosa Production), Gian Paolo Barbieri, Kendra Kabasele (Icon International), Sandra (Seed), Alexa Murray (Balcony Jump), Sabine Killinger (Elite Model Management), Cristina Palumbo (*Vogue* Italy), Luca Marchetti (West Artists Photographers Management), Peter Pugliese (CLM), Jessica Marx (Art and Commerce), Chloe Charlesworth (D and V Management), Lorenzo Bringheli, Christian Schuett (Bird Production).